Oliver Turner
a club in
2013 aged 9

St. Chads
church
thursday
7.00 - 8.00

cubs
Annual 2013

scouts
be prepared . . .

Stick in a photo of yourself here – or draw a self-portrait!

This annual belongs to:

Oliver Turner

I am .... 9 .... years old.

I belong to the ...... 16th ......

...... Sutton coldfield ... Cub Scout Pack.

I joined Scouting in 20 12 to 2013 ....

Scouts in 2014

Cub Scouts know the coolest stuff. Right?

But when I joined as a Cub Scout I felt like I didn't know a thing. All that changed when the leaders and other Cubs started to share their skills and knowledge with me. I remember one of the first things I did was to be given one match and one raw sausage and told to go and cook it. I remember looking at the match and looking at the sausage and thinking, it's going to have to burn for a very long time! Then someone showed me how to make a fire and I thought, wow, this is going to be fun!

The *Cubs Annual 2013* will teach you plenty of things that will amaze your friends. But remember to pass on what you learn. Life is much more fun when you share what you know; that's how friends are made. You'll find out how to write secret codes; you'll learn how to turn a full glass of water upside down without spilling a drop (I'm not kidding) and, best of all, you'll start to become a real outdoors expert. By the end you'll be able to tell the difference between a beech tree and an oak tree just by looking at the leaves. Do you know one cloud from the next? You will by 2014.

We've got stories about adventures on Everest (including mine); cool facts on how people learned to fly (with a little help from balloons and aeroplanes) and even ideas on how to make new toys from bits of old rubbish. It's amazing what you can do when you put your mind to it.

You'll find all this and more in the *Cubs Annual 2013*. Happy reading, and don't be afraid to get out there and start an adventure of your own!

Your friend,

Bear

Bear Grylls
Chief Scout

Contents

Tree-mendous!

Do you like climbing trees, kicking up leaves and searching for conkers? A day exploring the woods is brilliant fun. You can build a den, go on a leaf hunt, perhaps even camp out for a couple of nights. Read on to find out more about woods, forests and the trees that grow in them.

Do you recognize these common trees? Tick the box if you have seen the tree before.

There's nothing like being out and about in the woods and forests.

Oak ☐
Famous for producing acorns, the oak can live for hundreds of years.

Silver birch ☐
Its light silver trunk makes it stand out from the other trees.

Horse chestnut ☐
Famous for its shiny brown conkers and hand-shaped leaves.

Sycamore ☐
Look out for its large winged seeds, sometimes called 'helicopters', which are carried by the wind.

Beech ☐
Its triangular brown nuts are encased in a soft spiny coat.

Willow ☐
Sometimes called the weeping willow because of its drooping branches – great for hide and seek!

Terrific trees

Trees are really amazing. Did you know:

- They can live for thousands of years, much longer than most other living things. A spruce tree found growing in Sweden is thought to be 9,550 years old!
- There are more than 80,000 species of tree.
- Trees are among the biggest living things in the world. The largest known tree is a Giant Sequoia in California nicknamed 'General Sherman' (see right). It is about 83 metres high with a diameter of 7.7 metres!

Tree teasers

How much do you know about trees? Test yourself with this mini-quiz – look at page 5 to find the names of the six trees. (Answers on page 62.)

1 An acorn is the seed of which tree? . . . .

2 From which tree does a conker come? . . . .

3 Which tree grows a triangular-shaped nut? . . . .

4 Which tree has bark the colour of a precious metal? . . . .

5 Which tree produces spinning seeds that we sometimes call 'helicopters'? . . . .

6 People often say this tree is weeping because of its drooping branches . . . .

Why are trees so important?

Humans could not survive without trees. When we breathe in, our bodies take in oxygen and as we breathe out, we release another gas called carbon dioxide. Trees produce oxygen and remove the carbon dioxide from the air. Trees help us breathe!

Trees also provide food and shelter for many creatures. Birds build nests in their branches, small animals make homes in their trunks and other creatures survive on their seeds, nuts and fruits.

Trees and animals help each other. Squirrels, for example, collect acorns to eat. They bury some in the ground as a store of food for the winter. But sometimes the squirrels forget where they have buried their acorns! So what happens? The acorn eventually grows into an oak tree. The squirrel's poor memory keeps the woods growing!

Even when trees get older and begin to rot, the dead wood provides an important home for minibeasts.

Get that badge!

Exploring a forest, park or woodland can help you get your **Cub Scout Naturalist Activity Badge**.

Look at a log

Investigate a rotting log and you will find all kinds of fascinating minibeasts, such as woodlice, centipedes, millipedes and beetles. You can use a bug jar and a magnifying glass to inspect them more closely. Always be gentle and return the minibeasts to where you found them.

Let's go on a leaf hunt

Lots of ideas for things to do with the leaves you find.

Next time you go for a walk in the woods, look around for interesting leaves. Collect as many kinds of leaves as you can – look for different shapes, colours and textures. When you get home, try these fun leafy activities.

- **Do a leaf rubbing.** Place your leaf on a smooth surface and lay a piece of thin paper on top of it. Use coloured crayons to rub over the top of the paper. You should be able to see the outline and the veins of the leaf. Make lots of lovely leaf rubbings.

- **Make a leaf creature.** Glue a leaf to a sheet of paper, then glue on or draw extra features – legs, eyes, etc. – to make them into funny animals or weird monsters. You could even add a background behind your finished leaf creature.

- **Make leaf 'Snap!'** Collect pairs of similar-looking leaves (you can also use petals and flowers for more variety). Press the leaves between sheets of newspaper with a heavy book on top. After about a week they will be nice and flat. Count how many leaves you have. Now cut out one rectangle of card for every leaf. Glue your

leaves on to the cards and wait for them to dry. To make them last longer, you can cover them with sticky back plastic. Now play 'Snap!'

- **Make silhouette leaf art.** This is best done outside as it can be quite messy. Put plenty of newspaper down first. Place your leaf or leaves in a nice arrangement on to a large sheet of paper, then spatter paint on top of them with an old toothbrush and some liquid poster paint. Let it dry and take off the leaves to reveal some great silhouette leaf shapes.

Leaf quiz

Here are six leaves. Do you know which tree they belong to? Each leaf is from one of the six trees on page 5. Write the tree name in the space. Answers on page 62.

OAK

Silver BIRCH

Willow

BEECH

SYCAMORE

Horse CHESTNUT

8

Daring dens

Fallen branches, twigs and leaves can help you make a brilliant den or shelter. But remember – never cut down or break off a tree's branches. Use only those that have already fallen off the tree.

How to build your den:

1 First, find a suitable tree – it will need to have some low branches or a knobbly bit to wedge your first branch into. Find two longish branches. One of the branches will need to be fork shaped at one end. Arrange them carefully to form the base of your den.

2 Collect as many big branches as you can and lean them neatly against your base, making a kind of 'tent'.

3 To finish off your shelter, collect smaller branches, twigs and leaves and push them into the gaps between the branches. This will make a good roof.

Now your den is ready to play in!

Let's put on a show!

A show is a great way to get a party going or to liven up a camping trip.

Scouts all over the world often put on performances called 'gang shows'. The cast members will sing songs, tell jokes, do magic tricks or act something out. It feels really good to perform in front of an audience and hear them enjoying the show.

'I LIKE IT WHEN THE AUDIENCE LAUGHS AND CLAPS!'

Luke, Cub Scout, age 9

Super skits

'Skits' or stunts are very short, very silly performances that will have your Pack falling about laughing. Why not act out a skit of your own? Give this one a try – you'll need at least four people but the more the merrier!

The invisible bench

Cub 1 pretends to 'sit' on an invisible bench. Along comes Cub 2. He/she says: 'What are you doing?'

Cub 1: 'I'm sitting on an invisible bench. Would you like to join me?'

Cub 2: 'Yes, please.' He/she pretends to sit down next to the first Cub on the 'bench'.

Along comes Cub 3.

Cub 3: 'What are you doing?'

The two Cubs reply: 'We're sitting on an invisible bench, would you like to join us?'

Cub 3 sits down and the skit continues with Cubs 4, 5, and so on. Until it comes to the last Cub in the group who says: 'What are you doing?'

All the Cubs reply: 'Sitting on an invisible bench.'

Final Cub: 'No you're not, I sold it last week!'

At this, all the Cubs on the bench suddenly fall on to the floor!

Here are some more hilarious skits for you to try:

Rubbish

Cub 1 enters the stage and says loudly: 'Banana skins, empty cans, bottle tops, apple cores, sweet wrappers, mouldy cheese, juice cartons . . .' (and anything else he/she can think of).

Cub 2 enters and interrupts, saying: 'What are you doing?'

Cub 1 replies: 'I'm talking a load of old rubbish!'

Gotta go wee

Props: Chairs optional, or everyone can sit on the floor.

A group of Cubs sit down in rows as if they are on a bus or a coach. One person is the driver at the front. He/she pretends to steer the wheel and makes driving sounds.

Cub 1 jumps up and shouts: 'Driver, please stop the bus, I've gotta go wee!'

The driver says: 'I can't stop here. You'll have to wait. Please sit down.'

Cub 1 sits down, driver drives. A few seconds later Cub 1 jumps up again saying: 'Please, driver, can you stop the bus. I've gotta go wee!'

The driver says: 'It's not far now. Hold on a bit longer and we'll be there soon.'

Cub 1 sits down, driving continues. A few moments later Cub 1 jumps up again, saying: 'Please, driver. I've gotta go wee. I've really, really gotta go wee. Stop the bus!'

The driver looks cross and pretends to stop the bus: 'OK, I'm stopping the bus, out you go!'

Cub 1 pretends to jump off the bus. He runs around in a circle and shouts: 'WHEEEEEEEEEE!'

Why not try making up some funny 'skits' of your own?

Top tips for perfect performances

- **Rehearse** your act before you perform it, so that everyone taking part knows what they are supposed to be doing.
- **Speak up!** Say your lines loudly and clearly and don't talk too fast. You want your audience to hear what you're saying and not miss the funny punchline.
- When it is someone else's turn to speak, try to **keep still**. Don't whisper or wave to your friends, as it will distract the audience.
- **Enjoy yourself!** If you're having a good time, the audience will too.

Doctor! Doctor!

These jokes work really well if one Cub pretends to be the doctor and sits at a table. The other Cubs are the patients, who enter, say their line, and leave. The trick is to keep the jokes coming quickly, so that one patient comes in straight after the other has finished.

Patient: Doctor! Doctor! Everyone keeps ignoring me.
Doctor: Next!

Patient: Doctor! Doctor! I feel like a pair of curtains.
Doctor: Pull yourself together!

Patient: Doctor! Doctor! I keep thinking I'm a bridge.
Doctor: What's come over you today?

Patient: Doctor! Doctor! I keep thinking I'm a ladder.
Doctor: Let's take things one step at a time.

Patient: Doctor! Doctor! I keep thinking I'm a sheep.
Doctor: How do you feel?
Patient: Baaad. Really baaad.

Patient: Doctor! Doctor! I keep thinking I'm a dog.
Doctor: How long have you felt like this?
Patient: Ever since I was a puppy!

Patient: Doctor! Doctor! I've only got 59 seconds to live!
Doctor: Just a minute.

Patient: Doctor! Doctor! I feel like a cooked strawberry.
Doctor: Oh dear, you are in a jam.

How did 'gang shows' start?

In October 1932 the first ever gang show was held in London. The idea was to raise money to build a swimming pool for The Scout Association. The name 'gang show' came about because Ralph Reader, the organizer, asked one of the Scouts if he was ready to start rehearsing. He replied 'Aye, Skip – the gang's all here!'

Gang shows became a huge success. They were staged throughout the Second World War and were even attended by royalty. The gang show tradition goes on today and they are still a good way of raising money.

Get that badge!

Putting on a show could help you get a **Cub Scout Entertainer Badge** or **Cub Scout Creative Challenge Badge**. It could even help raise funds for your Group or for a charity. So get rehearsing!

Food always seems to taste better eaten outside.

Stick it on a stick

It's fun to cook a meal on a real fire – and even more fun to 'stick it on a stick' and toast your food over the glowing embers. What's more, you won't have any washing up to do afterwards! All you need is a campfire, some green sticks – and some tasty food, of course.

Grab a green stick

Ask your leader to cut you a thin fresh twig or branch. Your stick should be long enough for you to safely hold it over a fire without burning yourself.

Now (with adult supervision) strip the bark from the stick with a penknife. Hold the stick over the heat of the fire to dry out the sap. The sap will spoil your food if you don't do this.

Always use fresh twigs, not dead wood for cooking. Green sticks are less likely to catch fire and are more flexible. If you can't find one, soak a dry stick in water for an hour before cooking.

Go for the glow

Your leader will organize and light the campfire for your group. The best kind of fire for cooking is one that consists of glowing embers. This means that the fire needs to be lit a good while before cooking your meal. You can keep the embers hot at all times by adding small amounts of dry wood at regular intervals.

Egg on a stick

It might sound impossible, but you can cook an egg using just a green stick. Here's how!
1 Tap a small hole at each end of the egg (just big enough to push your stick through).
2 Carefully push your stick through the eggshell.
3 Hold the egg on a stick over the embers of the fire, turning now and again. In about five minutes, you will have a tasty cooked egg, ready to shell!

Cracking kebabs

Ingredients:

- Bacon
- Mushrooms
- Sausage
- Carrots
- Peppers
- A green stick

1 Thread slices of bacon, mushroom, sausage, carrot and peppers (and anything else that takes your fancy) on to your stick.

2 Hold or support your kebab over the embers, turning every now and again to make sure that your food is well cooked on all sides. Don't grill your kebab too fast: otherwise the meat will be brown on the outside but raw in the middle.

3 It's very important that your meat is cooked all the way through – when you think it is cooked, cut into it to check if it is still pink in the middle. If it is, continue cooking the meat for longer until all the pink has gone.

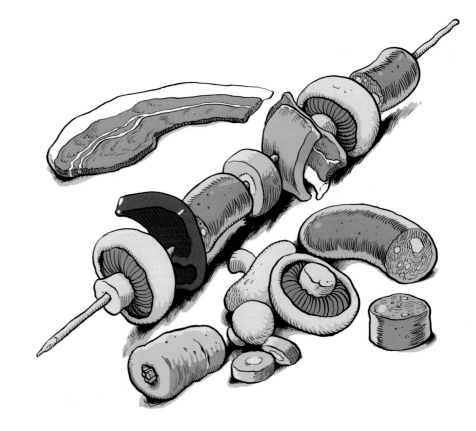

For dessert, why not try a delicious hot fruit kebab – chunks of apple, banana and orange work really well cooked on a stick. Be careful, it will be hot!

Snake on a stick

Sometimes called twists, these bread 'snakes' are fun to make and really good to eat.

Ingredients:

- Plain flour
- Water
- Salt
- A green stick

1 In a bowl, mix together flour, water and a pinch of salt to form a thick dough (or make the dough at home and bring it to camp with you). Don't put too much water in as it will make the dough too runny.

2 Take a piece of the dough and roll it into a 'snake'. Wrap the dough snake around a green stick and cook it over the embers, turning occasionally.

3 When cooked, these twists taste delicious with butter and jam or honey. You can also add raisins and sultanas to the dough for an even sweeter twist.

Super s'mores!

And finally, surely the yummiest campfire snack ever invented . . . s'mores! They taste so great that they will always leave you asking for 's'more'!

Ingredients (for each s'more)
- 2 marshmallows
- 2 chocolate digestive biscuits
- A green stick

1 Thread the marshmallows on the stick and toast them over the embers, until they are getting brownish on the outside but are still soft in the middle. Don't scoff just yet!

2 Use one of the biscuits to push the marshmallows off the stick and on to the other biscuit – chocolate side inwards!

3 Let the marshmallow melt the chocolate for a moment – now eat and enjoy!

Puppies in blankets

This is a delicious snack which uses the same dough as the snakes. You'll need frankfurter sausages, one for each person, as well as plenty of dough.

Ingredients:
- Frankfurter sausages
- Dough (as for snakes)
- A green stick

1 Put the sausage on a stick and warm it up over the fire.

2 Then, take a piece of dough and flatten it into a rectangle shape. Wrap it around the frankfurter and cook over the fire, turning occasionally. (You can also wrap a slice of cheese around the frankfurter first, if you like. It will melt – mmm.)

3 Finally, add ketchup to your 'puppy in a blanket' – and scoff!

Get that badge!

Preparing and clearing away an outdoor meal could help you get the **Cub Scout Camper Activity Badge.**

Use it again!

What a waste!

It's hard to imagine the huge amount of rubbish that gets thrown away every day. Food scraps, plastic bags, old clothes, videos, electrical appliances – the list goes on and on . . .

Much of the junk goes to places called landfill sites. It might be burnt, which can pollute the air, or buried, which takes up valuable space and can pollute the earth. But don't despair! There are lots of things you can do to help reduce the rubbish mountain.

Think of ways of reusing or recycling things. These days everybody has a recycling bin at home, but you can also take used things to your local recycling centre. Why not take your unwanted toys, books and clothes to the local charity shop or school fair, so that someone else can use them? Or make an unwanted object into something else?

Toy car made from old wire

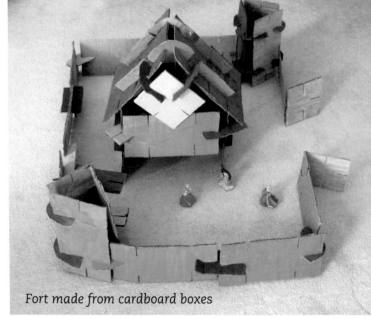
Fort made from cardboard boxes

Bracelets made from scrap paper

Get that badge!

Taking part in a recycling scheme and finding out about how we affect our environment can help you get a **Cub Scout Global Conservation Badge**.

16

Reduce your rubbish

Here are some simple ways of cutting down the stuff you usually throw away:

Brilliant bags

Say 'no thanks' to plastic carrier bags and get a reusable bag (or two) the next time you and your family go shopping. You could even suggest that your school or Pack looks into producing their own reusable bag with their special logo on the front. Why not help sell the bags to raise money at fairs and events?

Just one water bottle

Hundreds of empty plastic water bottles get thrown away every day. So get yourself a reusable water bottle, fill it up and take it out with you next time you go out to play. There are some great designs around with cool characters on them, flip tops that bounce up when pressed – even one with its own screw-on bug box!

Start composting

Compost is a dark crumbly fertilizer that is produced from decomposing (rotting) natural rubbish. It is great for your garden plants and it cuts down on waste. If you want to do some composting, ask your parent or guardian for help. Choose a corner of your garden that is quite far from the house to start a compost heap (it can be a bit stinky!) or get a special composting bin.

It will take a few months for all the scraps to turn into compost and you will need to turn the mixture with a spade now and again. When your compost heap is rich and brown, you can scatter the compost around the bottom of plants or mix it into the soil of potted plants. It will help them to grow and flourish.

Buy less packaging

Try to encourage your friends and family to buy foods that don't have too much packaging on them. For example, you could buy loose carrots and put them straight into your reusable bag, rather than packaged ones.

Things you can put in a compost heap or bin

- leaves, grass cuttings, dead flowers and similar garden waste

- fruit and vegetable scraps and peelings
- egg shells
- paper, cardboard, sawdust, animal manure – the bedding from a hamster's cage for example.

Do not put meat or fish scraps, wood, metal, glass or anything plastic in your compost!

Take a look at what one family managed to achieve:

The greenest family in Britain

The Strauss family from the Forest of Dean in England are recycling champions. They managed to cut down on waste so much that for a whole year, they only produced **one bag of rubbish**!

How did they do it? By buying only products with recyclable packaging, using their own bags for shopping and generally reusing everything as much as possible.

For example, eleven-year-old Verona loves crisps but she didn't want to throw away lots of individual crisp packets. To cut down on rubbish, her parents bought her one big bag of crisps per week and kept them in a lidded container. What a great idea!

Verona's bag holds the family's entire landfill waste for 2010 – containing items such as broken pens and negatives.

17

Make a lolly stick flyer

Don't throw away your used lolly sticks! Get recycling and make a fun flyer with them.

You will need:
- Six used lolly sticks
- Bowl of water

How to do it:

1 Soak the sticks in the bowl of water for five minutes. This will make them softer and easier to work with.

2 Take the sticks out and dry them. Lay three sticks out as shown here:

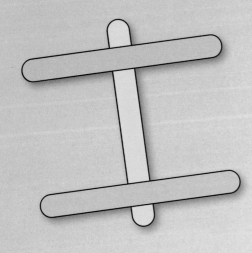

3 Take another two sticks and lay them across the others like this:

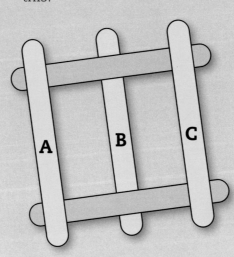

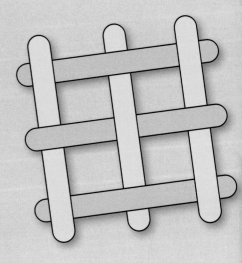

4 Here comes the tricky bit. Take the last stick and weave it over stick A, under stick B and over stick C. Don't worry if it all falls apart while you're doing it – just start again.

5 When your sticks are tightly woven together you are ready for a test flight. Go outside. Now skim your flyer through the air like a frisbee and see how far it goes. Whee!

Make gift tags from old cards

2 Place the glass on top of a picture you like and draw around the base with a pencil to get a perfect circle. Carefully cut out the picture to make a circular tag.

3 Punch a hole through the top of the tag – take care with this part as it's easy to punch the hole too close to the edge!

You will need:
- Unwanted birthday and Christmas cards
- Scissors
- Pencil
- Drinking glass
- Hole puncher
- Thread or ribbon

How to do it:

1 Sort through all your cards and choose ones that have nice small pictures or images on the front, such as stars, Santas, animals, etc. Look at the back of the pictures to make sure there is no writing on them.

Have you got any good ideas for reusing things that are normally thrown away? Describe your idea here:

4 Cut a short length of thread or ribbon (used gift ribbon is good), push it through the hole and tie it. You have made a gift tag!

Important: Don't forget to put the left over scraps of card and carton in a recycling box!

19

Scouts get busy!

Discover what Cubs and Beavers around the country have been getting up to!

Pitching for the Prime Minister

In the summer of 2011 a group of Cubs and Beavers earned themselves a unique badge – by camping out in the garden of 10 Downing Street, the home of the Prime Minister!

The fifteen proud boys and girls were from the Broomwood Beaver Colony of the 12th/14th Battersea Westside Scout Group. For some of the Beavers, the camping trip was their first night away from home.

The lucky group got a tour inside the Number Ten building, then went outside to play games, cook meals and bed down for the night. They also raised money for the children's health charity Sparks.

They even had a badge specially designed for them. It features the world-famous 'Number Ten' black door.

'WHEN I FOUND OUT WE WERE GOING TO DOWNING STREET, I COULDN'T BELIEVE IT!'

Thomas, Beaver Scout, 8

Where would you like to camp if you could put your tent up anywhere in the world?

Name that shark

Cub Scout Ewan and his Pack, from Fife, in Scotland, made a special visit to the **Deep Sea World** Aquarium to meet a Sand Tiger Shark. Ewan had won a competition organized by The Scout Association and the aquarium to give the shark a name. Can you guess what the winning name was? Scout!

Scouting for everyone

It's always exciting when a new Scout Group is set up, but no one could be more excited than the children of Saxon Hill School in Staffordshire. They are all girls and boys who have additional needs and disabilities. Enjoying outdoor activities can be more challenging than usual – but that hasn't stopped them! Since 2010 they have been camping on the school grounds, cooked on open fires, enjoyed campfire songs and have even been up a climbing wall in harnesses.

Time-travelling Beavers

The 1st Wivenhoe Beaver Scout Colony buried a time capsule. They are hoping that in 25 years' time a future Beaver Colony will open it up and see what it was like to be a Beaver 'in the past'. Inside the capsule were:

- letters the Beavers had written about things we have now that we didn't have 25 years ago
- a selection of Beaver Scout badges
- photos of places the Colony had visited

The capsule was covered by a concrete slab and every Beaver in the Colony put in their initial and their thumbprint.

Cranes for charity

When a tsunami devastated Japan in 2011, Eugene, a Cub Scout from Woking, decided to do something practical to help. So he began making origami cranes to raise money, helped by his brother Kai.

Eugene and Kai sold their cranes to the local Scout and Guides, as well as at school and in the community. The paper birds proved very popular and the brothers raised over £3,500 for the British Red Cross Japan Tsunami Appeal. What an amazing achievement!

Would you like to know how to make an origami crane? Then turn over the page.

Would you like to know how to make an origami crane? Then turn over the page.

Get that badge!

Helping with an event that raises money for charity could help you get a **Cub Scout Community Challenge Badge.**

Community

21

Make an origami crane

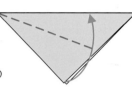

Origami is the Japanese art of paper folding. Origami experts can make amazing birds, animals and fish – just like these.

The most famous origami model is the crane – a sacred Japanese bird which is also a symbol of peace around the world. In Japan every child learns how to make this crane.

An ancient Japanese legend says that anyone who folds a thousand origami cranes will be granted a wish!

You will need:

- A piece of origami paper. Or use a piece of thin A4 paper, with the top cut off, to make a square.

Tip: Make sure you crease all your folds really well.

How to do it:

1 Place the origami paper colour side down on a table. Turn the square so that a corner is at the top. Fold it in half so that the top point meets the bottom point, and crease.

2 You now have a triangle. Fold the left edges upwards, so that they meet the top edge, and crease.

3 Fold the edges over towards you, like this, and crease.

4 Take the left corner of the triangle and fold it at an angle to the right, like this. This is the crane's neck.

5 Take the top of the neck and fold it towards the left. This is the head.

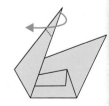

6 You've made a crane!

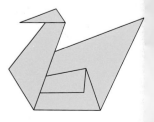

22

14 things to do before you're 14

The Scout Association and the Discovery Channel have made a list of activities and skills that they think would be useful for young people to know.

How many of these things can you do? Tick the box if it's a yes.

Don't worry if you can't tick many boxes – you have got plenty of time. Leave the other boxes blank so that you can tick them off in the future.

> **'HAVING THESE SKILLS HELPS YOUNG PEOPLE PREPARE FOR WHATEVER LIFE THROWS AT THEM.'**
>
> *Bear Grylls*

1	Navigate using a map	☐
2	Climb a tree	✓
3	Make and fly a kite	✓
4	Cook a meal	☐
5	Repair a bike	✓
6	Camp outdoors with your friends	✓
7	Build a den	✓
8	Put up a tent	✓
9	Ride a sledge	✓
10	Use a telescope to look at the stars	✓
11	Light a fire safely	✓
12	Learn basic first aid	✓
13	Go on a nature trail	✓
14	Tie a reef knot	✓

What other things could you add to the list of things to do before you are 14? Catch a fish? Do a skateboard trick?

If you haven't ticked number 14 – the reef knot – here's how to do it.

Tie a reef knot

1 Take an end of the string or rope in each hand and lay the left-hand end over the right.

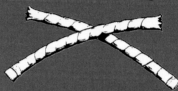

2 Then, using your right hand, take the end from the left down behind the other rope and up to the front again.

3 Point the ends inwards again, this time the right-hand end over the other one, then take it down behind it and up to the front, through the loop which has now been formed.

4 Pull the knot tight – and keep practising.

Have you tried . . . ?

Here's a selection of exciting Scouting activities. Do you know what they all are? Can you match the activities to the right definitions?

HIGH ROPES

3G SWING

ORIENTEERING

ROLLERBLADING

TRAMPOLINING

ROWING

CAMPING

1 Get hauled up into the air –
   then pull the cord and swing
   at high speed!

2 It's fun to bounce, jump and do
   acrobatics on this super-springy
   surface.

3 Ask your leader when your
   Pack will spend a night away.

4 Whizzing along on tiny wheels
   is brilliant, but be sure to wear a
   helmet and knee pads in case of
   scrapes.

5 Find your way around a special
   route using a map – it's a bit like
   a treasure hunt. First back wins!

6 An exciting challenge in which
   you climb and jump your way
   though a rope course, wearing a
   harness and helmet.

   High

7 Pull the oars to move your boat
   through the water, either solo or
   with a team.

   rowing

   Which of these activities
   would you like to try?

Answers on page 62

25

My first camp

There's no better way to experience the great outdoors than under canvas.

Are you about to spend your very first night camping? If so, you are in for the time of your life. Here are some tips to help make your adventure the coolest ever!

What to expect

If you're a Cub Scout, your leader will organize the camping trip for the group, so you won't need to worry about taking all the tents, camping equipment and food. You'll simply need to get permission from your parents, take in your form and pack a bag. Some first-time camping trips take place inside or outside halls or at a Scout meeting place, others could be in a garden, field or wood. You might help with putting up tents and you will certainly be asked to help out with tasks such as tidying up and perhaps preparing food.

Wherever you end up camping, you can expect to stay up later than usual, play lots of games, eat some very tasty food and have fun with all your friends!

Perfect packing

Try not to take too much with you. Not only will your bag be heavy to carry, the more stuff you take, the more difficult it will be to find the things you really want. As you pack, ask yourself 'Do I really need this?' Use a sturdy rucksack or bag – the type with lots of outer pockets is great for things like water bottles, which might leak inside. Put the things you need the most at the top, like pyjamas.

Camping essentials

- A hooded waterproof mac and a change of clothes in case you get wet – even in summer.

- Strong outdoor shoes or boots that will keep your feet dry.

- Tissues or wet wipes.

- Bottle of water.

- Snack – food will be provided but it's always good to have a favourite cereal bar or some fruit in case you feel peckish.

- Warm pyjamas and a washbag containing flannel, soap, toothbrush and toothpaste. Antiseptic hand gel is also a good idea.

- Any special medicines or creams you may need.

- Clean clothes – including underwear – for the next morning.

- Torch – wind-up ones won't run out of batteries.

- Your own plastic or metal plate, bowl, cup and cutlery.

- Sunscreen and sunhat if the weather is hot.

- A tea towel.

- A couple of empty plastic carrier or bin bags – great for taking home dirty clothes and wet shoes.

Keep cosy

Even in the summer, it can get really cold when the sun goes down. So make sure you bring a warm sleeping bag. The light type of bag that you might use for a sleepover at a friend's house will probably not be warm enough for outdoors. Most sleeping bags have warmth ratings – make sure yours is high enough to keep you toasty all through the night! And don't forget a pillow!

You will also need a sleeping mat to put under your sleeping bag. This will keep you comfy by providing insulation between you and the ground.

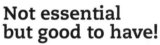

Not essential but good to have!

- Things to play with e.g. a frisbee, a blow-up ball, a pack of cards. Don't take electronic games – they're not good for group activities and you will be so busy you won't have time to play with them anyway.
- Binoculars – great for looking at the landscape and night-time stargazing.
- A favourite toy or teddy to cuddle up with in your sleeping bag.

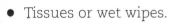

Get that badge!

Spending the night camping or on a sleepover, and learning outdoor skills, can help you gain some great badges, including the **Cub Scout Camper Activity Badge and the Staged Nights Away Badges.**

Be a considerate camper

- Listen to your leader's instructions and follow them. Respect camp rules such as bedtime.
- Help to tidy and clear up camp. You should leave the land just as you found it, taking home any rubbish to dispose of.
- Stay away from fields of crops or farm animals.
- Never wander off on your own – always stick with your fellow Cubs.

The hazards of camping – a funny poem

Did no one ever tell you
When you first arrived at camp,
That it's not the early rising
Or the spiders, or the damp,
The spooky rustling of the trees
Or suffering from the cramp
That wakes you with a ghastly fright
And keeps you up all through the night?

No, it's finding that your tent-mate
Snores his head off every night!

Rock that camp!

Have a blast on your next camping trip!

Have a camp yell: Ham and Eggs

Have fun calling out the lines together. Split the group into two for this yell.

First half: **'Ham and eggs'**
Second half: **'Ham and eggs'**
First half: **'I like mine done nice and brown'**
Second half: **'I like mine done upside down'**
First half: **'Flip 'em'**
Second half: **'Flop 'em'**
First half: **'Flip 'em'**
Second half: **'Flop 'em'**
All together: **'HAM – AND – EGGS!'**

Have a scavenger hunt

Ask your leader to write down a list of items for everyone to find and bring back to camp. Work in pairs to run off and find the objects. The first pair back with all the items wins. The leader should place a time limit – ten minutes or so – on the hunt.

Things to find
- Something red (or any other colour) – this could be an item of clothing, a strawberry, a flower, a ladybird . . .
- A forked twig
- Something smooth
- A seed
- Something you can eat
- Something prickly
- A pine cone
- A pebble

Play an outdoor game: Hot and Cold

You will need:
- A scarf for the blindfold

How to play

1 One person volunteers to be blindfolded. When he/she has the blindfold on, the leader silently chooses a nearby object or location (this could be a tree, a rucksack, a gate, etc.) to be the finishing point.

2 Now, the rest of the group has to guide the blindfolded person to the location by calling out 'Hot' or 'Cold'. The blindfolded person begins to move and if he/she moves nearer to the location, everyone calls out 'Hot'. If he/she moves further away, call out 'Cold'.

This is great fun to play – you can even have several players in blindfolds and do it as a relay. Or split the group into two teams and each team shouts at their own player. This causes chaos as the 'blind' players try to work out which shouts they should be listening to!

Choc-a-block!

Do you like chocolate? We're guessing you do – so read on to find out more about this tasty treat.

It's one of the nation's favourite snacks. A s'more wouldn't be the same without it (see page 15 for the recipe). But where does chocolate come from? And how is it made?

The story of chocolate

- More than two thousand years ago, the Ancient Mayans were one of the first to discover the cocoa tree. They took the cocoa beans from the tree's pods and ground them up into a paste. It was mixed with spices and water to make a thick bitter drink – nothing like today's delicious hot chocolate!
- Cocoa was a favourite of the Aztec Emperor Montezuma, who is said to have drunk up to 50 cups of 'xocoatl' a day. The Aztecs liked cocoa so much that they even used cocoa beans as coins!
- Cocoa was introduced into Britain during the seventeenth century but bars of chocolate didn't appear until Victorian times. Fry & Sons made the first bar using cocoa powder and sugar. It was rather dry and bitter, not like today's chocolate.
- The Swiss had the bright idea of adding condensed milk to the cocoa, which made the chocolate taste creamy and delicious. By 1905 full cream milk chocolate could be bought in the shops. One of the bars on sale was the famous 'Dairy Milk', made by Cadbury, which you can still buy today.

From bean to bar

All chocolate begins with cocoa beans. The beans are found in the pods of the cocoa

Cocoa beans and a cocoa pod

tree, which grows best in hot, rainy conditions. Each cocoa pod contains between 20 and 40 beans. They look like fat almonds cocooned in cotton wool.

The beans are scooped out of the pods and put in piles to ferment while the flavour develops. Then the beans are dried and taken to factories where they are roasted and crushed. The outer shell is thrown away while the inner kernels – called cocoa nibs – are crushed into a thick substance called cocoa liquor. This grainy paste is blended with sugar, milk powder and other flavours such as vanilla.

After the mixture has been stirred and mixed by machine, it becomes lovely liquid chocolate and can be made into the bars and treats that we see in the shops.

Sweet secrets

One of the most famous stories about chocolate is called *Charlie and the Chocolate Factory*, by the author Roald Dahl. In the story, Charlie Bucket is so poor that he only gets one bar of chocolate a year on his birthday – so he eats it very slowly to make the most of it.

Charlie eventually meets the famous Willy Wonka, who owns the local chocolate factory. Mr Wonka keeps his factory top-secret as he is very worried about spies stealing his secret recipes.

But did you know that in real life, chocolate spies actually existed? Back in the 1920s, Cadbury and Rowntree, two famous chocolate manufacturers, tried to find out each other's chocolate making secrets by sending spies (pretending to be workers) into each other's factories!

Crunchy chocolate fridge cake

This delicious cake is easy to make and, best of all, doesn't need any baking. It's ideal to take away on a camping trip. Just wrap it up in foil and enjoy when you're ready for a sweet treat.

What you need – equipment:
- An adult helper
- Cake tin
- Foil
- Mixing bowl & wooden spoon
- Saucepan

Ingredients:
- 100g dark or plain chocolate
- 2 tablespoons double cream
- 200g plain biscuits – digestive or rich tea are good
- 100g butter
- A handful of raisins
- Optional: other chopped dried fruits such as apricots or cherries.

How to do it:

1 Wash your hands and prepare the cake tin by carefully pressing a large piece of foil into it. Make sure there are no holes or tears in the foil and that it is large enough to cover the top of the cake when you have finished.

2 Break the biscuits into the mixing bowl using your fingers. Keep on snapping them until you have lots of little pieces.

3 For this part you will need an adult helper. Break the chocolate into squares and place into a saucepan. Stir over a very low heat until the chocolate has melted. Add the butter and cream and stir in.

4 Pour the chocolate mixture on to the biscuits and stir it up all together with a wooden spoon. Add the raisins and mix them in.

5 Spoon the mixture into the foil lined cake tin. Cover it up with the foil edges.

6 Place the cake in the fridge for around two hours or until it is nice and firm. Unwrap the foil, cut into pieces and eat! Mmmm.

Food Funnies

What stands in the middle of Paris and wobbles like a jelly? *The Trifle Tower.*

Which vegetable should you never take on a boat? *A leek.*

Feast on these tasty yet terrible jokes!

What jam can't be eaten on toast? *A traffic jam.*

What is a monkey's favourite snack? *Chocolate chimp cookies!*

Why did the biscuit cry? *Because its mother had been a wafer so long.*

What do pixies eat at parties? *Fairy cakes.*

What's white, fluffy and beats its chest in a cake shop? *A meringue-utang.*

What did the astronaut say when he stepped on a chocolate bar? *'I have just set foot on Mars!'*

Which is the strongest vegetable? *The muscle sprout.*

How do you make a sausage roll? *Push it down a hill.*

What tables can you eat? *Vegetables!*

What do you call a Scout with a massive box of chocolates? *Popular!*

'Magic' science

Impress your friends with these mind-boggling experiments.

Bubble magic

You will need:
- Bubble mixture
- Crushed ice
- A plastic bottle
- A dish

How to do it:

1 Pour the bubble mixture into the dish.

2 Put the crushed ice inside the bottle. Now put the lid on the bottle and shake it. The air inside will cool down.

3 Take the lid off the bottle. Tip the ice out and also any water that is now in the bottle.

4 Dip the open end of the bottle into the bubble mixture so that it is covered with an unbroken film of bubble mixture.

5 Leave the bottle standing upright. Now watch what happens as the air inside the bottle begins to warm up again.

How does it work?

Air is made up of tiny parts called molecules that are constantly moving. As air warms up, the molecules move around faster and bump into each other. They need more space so the air expands and rises up into the bubble mixture, which makes the bubble. This is how hot air balloons rise up, up and away!

The non-spill glass

Can you turn a glass of water upside down – without the water pouring out? Here's how to do it.

You will need:
- A drinking glass
- Water
- A piece of thin card (an old cereal box works well)
- Scissors

How to do it:

1 Cut the card so that you have a piece about 2cm wider than the rim of the glass.

2 Slowly fill the glass to the top

The jumping coin

Make the coin jump as if by magic!

You will need:

- A bowl of ice-cold water
- A 2p coin
- A glass bottle – check that the opening is smaller than the coin

How to do it:

1 Place the neck of the bottle and the coin into the bowl of cold water for a couple of minutes to chill them. Make sure you don't get any water into the bottle.
2 Place the coin on the top of the bottle opening, without any gaps between the bottle and the coin.
3 Wrap your hands around the bottle and wait to see what happens!

How does it work?

When you hold the bottle with your warm hands, the air inside the bottle heats up. The warm air expands and pushes its way out of the bottle, forcing the coin to 'jump'.

with water. The water should be exactly level with the top of the glass. Be careful!

3 Do this next stage over a sink – just in case! Put the card on top of the glass so that it is like a lid. Hold the card to the glass with your hand and carefully turn the glass upside down.
4 Now slowly take your hand away and the water should stay in the glass, with the card holding it in as if by magic!

How does it work?

Because the glass is full, there is no air in the glass to push the water out. The card sticks to the surface of the water. If you take the card away from the glass you will let air in and the water will pour out as it is pushed out by the air.

Get that badge!

Performing experiments like the ones here can help you get your **Cub Scout Scientist Badge** and your **Cub Scout Entertainer Badge**.

Have you tried . . . ?

Here's a selection of exciting Scouting activities. Do you know what they all are? Can you match the activities to the right definitions?

ICE SKATING

CLIMBING WALL

MOUNTAIN BIKING

HIKING

SKIING

GEOCACHING

SKATEBOARDING

1 Get moving on your board, then try tricks like ollies and flips!

2 Very slippery at first, but you should soon get your balance on the ice and gain confidence.

3 Grab on to a hold and get a good foothold. Then push yourself up and try to reach the top.

4 Can you find the hidden containers ('caches')? You'll have a GPS device or a smartphone to help you.

5 Rough and ready cycling on outdoor tracks and trails. It can be muddy!

6 You need plenty of snow for this sport but once you've mastered it, you'll be whizzing down the slopes in no time.

7 You'll need sturdy shoes for this energetic outdoor walk. Choose your own route or follow a trail – and enjoy the scenery.

Which of these activities would you like to try next?

Answers on page 62

Keep it secret!

Would you and your friends like to exchange secret messages?

Secret codes and ciphers have been around for many hundreds of years. In ancient times, when letters were carried by messengers, important messages were often written in code so that only a few people 'in the know' could understand them. This is called 'encryption'. Today, encryption is used for all kinds of information that is stored in computers. The method is much more advanced but the idea is still the same – to keep information private.

Send a secret message

One way of sending a secret message is to use something called a 'cipher'. In a cipher, the letters of your message are replaced by different letters, numbers or symbols. Here are lots of ideas for ciphers that you and your friends can share.

The rod cipher

You will need:

- Two identical rods – two pencils work well
- A thin strip of paper, 1–2 cm wide

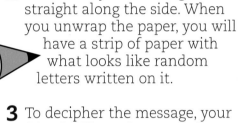

How to do it:

1 Wrap the paper strip around the pencil.

2 Now write your message straight along the side. When you unwrap the paper, you will have a strip of paper with what looks like random letters written on it.

3 To decipher the message, your friend will need to wrap the paper around his or her pencil. But the pencil must be the same size as yours!

Reverse the words

This is a very easy cipher. All you have to do is to write each word of your message backwards.

For example: **Meet me by the gate**

becomes **Teem em yb eht etag**

Can you write a reverse message to your friend?

A belt and a battle

Did you know that a cipher once helped win a war? In 405 BC a Greek general called Lysander of Sparta received a message that was written on the inside of a belt. When Lysander wound the belt around a wooden stick, the message was revealed. It told him that the Persians were about to attack. Lysander had time to gather his troops and sail off to defeat them!

A	B	C	D	E	F	G	H	I	J	K	L	M	N	O	P	Q	R	S	T	U	V	W	X	Y	Z
Z	Y	X	W	V	U	T	S	R	Q	P	O	N	M	L	K	J	I	H	G	F	E	D	C	B	A

Reverse the alphabet

In this cipher, each letter of the alphabet represents a different letter. All you have to do is write out two alphabets, the first the usual way, the second below it, but in reverse.

A stands for Z, B stands for Y and so on.

So **SCOUT**

would be **HXLFG**

Now write your own message here:

XFYH ZIV TIVZG!

What does the message above say?

Write it here:

Answer on page 62

A	B	C	D	E	F	G	H	I	J	K	L	M	N	O	P	Q	R	S	T	U	V	W	X	Y	Z
1	2	3	4	5	6	7	8	9	10	11	12	13	14	15	16	17	18	19	20	21	22	23	24	25	26

Numbers for letters

In this cipher, a number replaces a letter. Each letter of the alphabet can be written alongside the numbers 1–26.

So **I love camping**

becomes

9 – 12 15 22 5 – 3 1 13 16 9 14 7

(You can separate the words with a dash.)

Now try writing your own number messages:

The Pigpen Code

This famous code was first used over one hundred years ago, during the American Civil War. You write out the alphabet in two grids, like this:

AB	CD	EF
GH	IJ	KL
MN	OP	QR

ST
UV WX
YZ

Each letter is shown by using the part of the 'pigpen' diagram around it. If it is the second letter in the box, then it has a dot in the middle.

Try using the pigpen code to write a message of your own.

So **A** looks like this:
And **B** looks like this:

Can you read this message?

Answer on page 62

Wartime secrets

In times of war, it is vital that top-secret information does not fall into enemy hands. Ciphers are often used for important messages. The trick is to know how to decipher the message! This can be very difficult. Code breakers are very skilled but they must also be very patient, as the work can take a long time.

During World War II (1939–1945), the Germans sent information to each other using a special machine which they called **Enigma**. It looked a bit like a typewriter with wheels and cogs – and it could scramble messages in over 150 million million million different ways! No wonder it was hard to crack. In fact, the Germans believed that Enigma's secrets could never be revealed. But though it seemed an impossible task, after several years of hard work, British code-breakers did work it out! Finding out about the enemy's plans helped the Allies gain victory in the war.

Get that badge!

Writing three simple messages using ciphers could help you get a **Cub Scout Communicator Activity Badge**. Why not use the ciphers in this book?

40

'My adventures as a spy'

It is very important for spies to be able to exchange messages, while keeping their contents secret. Lord Robert Baden-Powell, the founder of the Scouting movement, knew a lot about the world of secret agents. He had a long military career, experienced several wars and, at one point, worked as an intelligence officer – aka a spy.

Baden-Powell wrote a book called *My Adventures as a Spy* which was published in 1915. It tells of his experiences and is full of advice and adventure.

Baden-Powell during the Boer War in South Africa

Secret signs

In one chapter he gives tips on leaving secret signs for finding hidden messages. These signs are still used today for tracking in the woods.

This little mark, scratched on the ground or on a tree trunk or gate-post, was used by one Scout for the information of another. It means **'A letter is hidden four paces in this direction.'**

This is a sign used to warn another Scout that he is following a wrong direction. It means **'Not this way.'**

This is another sign from one Scout to another and means **'I have returned home.'**

Flying forts!

Another spy skill of Lord Baden-Powell's was that of disguise. He sometimes dressed up as a butterfly collector, and was able to investigate military forts in Germany, Tunisia and Algeria in this way. He would draw detailed sketches of the butterflies – but hidden in their wings were secret diagrams of each fort.

Spy games

Baden-Powell also says in the book that the game of Hide-and-Seek is very good practice for becoming a spy. It teaches you how to conceal yourself cleverly and to 'freeze' – to keep still, without a movement.

'I found it out long ago by lying flat along the top of an ivy-clad wall when my pursuers passed within a few feet of me without looking up at me.'

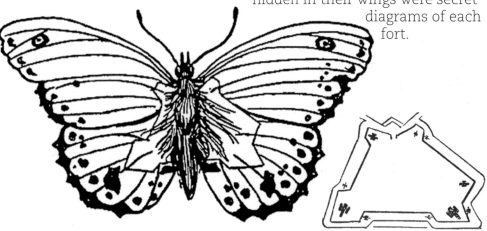

Would you make a good SPY?

Do you fancy yourself as a secret agent? Try this fun quiz to see if you have got what it takes.

1 A good spy notices details about people and places. She or he must also have an excellent memory. Test yourself by looking at this picture for a minute, then cover the picture up and answer the questions below. No peeking! Give yourself one point for every question you get right.

1 How many suitcases does the lady in the hat have? _____

2 Is the poodle in the picture on a lead?   YES / NO

3 What is the man wearing glasses doing? _____

4 How many pigeons are there in the picture? _____

5 The man with a moustache is wearing a scarf. Can you remember what colour it is?

_____

(5 points in total)

2 Spies are good communicators. In fact, many secret agents can speak other languages. Can you say any words in another language? Try matching the words below to their English meanings.

(French) *Bonne nuit*   **excuse me**

(German) *Danke*   **goodnight**

(Spanish) *Perdon*   **great**

(Italian) *Fantastico*   **thank you**

Get a point for every correct match (4 points in total).

3 Spies keep information secret. Can you write this message in a secret cipher? (See pages 38–40 for some ideas.)

MEET ME LATER.

Get 5 points if you can do it.

4 Spies might leave secret messages. What sign could you leave in the woods to show that you have returned home? (Tip – look back at page 41.)

Get 2 points for a correct answer.

5 Spies sometimes use special words for their spying activities. Would you know what a spy is talking about if he or she used the following words? Match them up.

a bug   a place where a spy can hide out

shadowing   a false name

safehouse   a secret listening device

a cover   secretly following someone

Get a point for every correct match. (4 points in total.)

Answers on page 62

How did you score?
15–20 points

You are a Super-Duper Spy! Your cover won't get blown easily! You can keep a cool head in a sticky situation and you're a great communicator. Keep up the good work, secret agent.

8–15 points

You are a Semi-Serious Spy! You've certainly got some serious spying skills – but you're not quite ready to be a full-on secret agent. Keep observing everyday details around you and you'll soon achieve Super-Duper Spy status.

Less than 8 points

You are a Slightly Sloppy Spy! It's back to spy school for you! You will need to do a lot of work before you're ready to become a secret agent. Writing secret messages to your friends is a good start.

Clever cloud-spotting

If you're off on a hike or about to set up camp, the more you know about the weather, the better.

Cumulus

Anyone can get the weather forecast from the newspapers, TV, radio or online but you can also tell a lot by looking around you – especially at the clouds above you. Looking carefully at a cloud's shape, size and texture can help you make a good guess at what is going to happen with the weather.

Take a look at the cloud descriptions below. It might even save you from getting wet!

Basic cloud types

Clouds can be sorted by their shape, how high they are in the sky, how big they are and how they are formed. There are four basic categories:

Cumulus clouds are puffy and look a bit like cotton wool balls, piled up on top of each other. They often indicate fair weather but if they are large and grey, there's a good chance of rain.

Stratus clouds are like a big sheet or blanket that can cover most of the sky. They hang low in the sky but as they are thin they don't usually produce a lot of rain or snow. Fog is actually very low-lying stratus cloud.

Stratus

Cirrus

What is a cloud?

A cloud is a large collection of tiny drops of water or ice crystals. Clouds form when humid air cools down enough for water vapour to condense.

Cirrus clouds are thin and wispy, like delicate tails or feathers. They are so high up that they are made of ice crystals and don't usually produce rain. But they can indicate a change in the weather.

Nimbus clouds bring rain and the name is often combined with other cloud types to show that they are rain clouds.

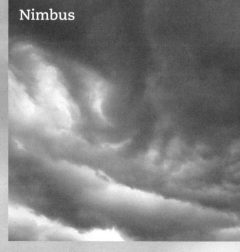

Nimbus

Look up!

Take a look outside. Can you spot any of these cloud types in the sky?

Altocumulus: Medium level clouds with a patchy, dappled appearance. They do not make much rain. The 'lumps' are larger and darker than cirrocumulus.

Cumulonimbus: A bigger, darker version of a cumulus cloud, with a cauliflower appearance. It will bring rain and maybe thunderstorms and hailstones.

Stratocumulus: Low clouds covering much of the sky, with a lumpy appearance. Probably no change in the weather and not much chance of rain, only drizzle.

Altostratus: Medium level clouds that usually cover the sky but let the sun shine through in a 'fuzzy' way. Expect weather to gradually worsen as these clouds may signal a later rainstorm.

Nimbostratus: Dark grey sheet of layered cloud – often bringing steady and long lasting rain.

Cirrostratus: Very high thin shapeless cloud covering the whole sky and sometimes producing a halo effect around the moon or the sun. Rain or snow may be on its way.

Cirrocumulus: High rippled clouds that look a bit like scales of a fish – which is why they are sometimes called a 'mackerel sky'. Often seen in winter when it is dry but cold.

Make a rain stick

Rain, rain go away Come again another day!

When you're outdoors having fun, the sight of rain clouds approaching is usually met with lots of moans and groans. But in some parts of the world, rain is welcomed – and even celebrated!

Legend has it that the people living in the dry deserts of Chile invented the rain stick to try to persuade their gods to make rainy weather. A rain stick is a tube filled with seeds or pebbles which makes a rattling sound – a bit like rain falling on leaves – when shaken. In Chile, a rain stick is traditionally made from a dead cactus tube. Cactus spines are hammered into the inside of the tube and it is then filled with tiny pieces of lava rock. In different cultures, rain sticks can be filled with things like pebbles, hard seeds, beans, sand, rice, or even tiny shells. But they are always used to encourage the skies to rain!

You can make your own rain stick using materials found around the house.

You will need:

- A long cardboard tube (the middle of a paper towel roll is ideal)
- Tinfoil
- Rice, lentils or unpopped popcorn
- Stiff paper
- Glue/sticky tape
- Scissors
- Paper to cover/decorations

How to do it:

1 Draw around the end of your tube on to the stiff paper. Do this twice.

2 Draw a bigger circle about 1–2cm around the first circle.

3 Draw lines about 1–2cm apart between the two circles, like spokes on a wheel. Cut out the big circle.

4 Cut along these lines (not too far in) and bend them. You have now made a lid for your tube. Glue/tape the lid securely over the end of the tube. Repeat the process to make a second lid and keep it for later.

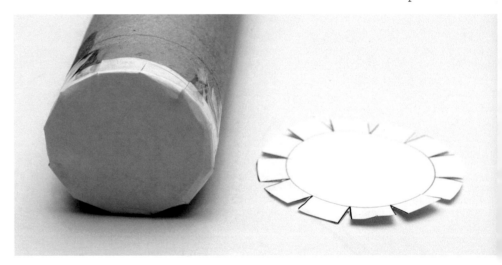

Rain facts

- Tropical rainforests are warm, wet forests with tall trees. They are bursting with life, being home to millions of different plants, animals and insects. Tropical rainforests are found in parts of the world which are close to the Equator, such as South America, West Africa and Southeast Asia. It rains a lot in these forests – sometimes 24 hours a day!

- When the sun shines on a rainy day, you might be lucky enough to see a rainbow. Sunlight is actually made up of different colours, which together normally appear as 'white' light. As sunlight passes through the rain's water droplets, it is bent and split so that we can see all the colours of the rainbow. Beautiful!

Turn your rain stick gently around – you will hear the sound of the rain as the lentils pour slowly though the foil twists. You can also use your rain stick as a fun musical instrument to accompany a song!

5 Now cut two pieces of tinfoil about 8cm longer than your tube.

6 Roll each piece up like a snake and then twist. Join your two twists together at the top and make a 'chain' shape by twisting them around each other.

7 Place the twist inside your tube. If there is a lot of space, make another twist and put that in too.

8 Now fill your rain stick (not too much, less than a quarter full is fine), with lentils, unpopped popcorn or rice.

9 Take your second circle lid and glue/ tape it securely over the other end of the tube.

10 Now for the fun part – decorate your rain stick by painting it or covering it with brightly coloured paper, drawings and decorations.

● Earthworms love the rain! Have you ever noticed that worms come out when it has been raining? It is usually too dry above ground for worms to survive but, after rain, the damp air helps the worms breathe and keep them moist.

47

Herbs are easy to grow and they taste great. What's more, you don't need a big garden – you can grow them indoors.

How does your garden grow?

A heavenly herb garden

You will need:
- **Containers for your herbs.** Any kinds of pots will do – even washed out yogurt containers. The pots will need small holes in the bottom to allow the water to drain through. Ask an adult to help make the holes.
- **A tray.** Put all your pots together in a tray to create your garden. The tray also catches the water from the pots.
- **A selection of herb seeds.** Choose herbs that don't grow too wide or tall. Chives, basil, lavender, parsley, mint and thyme are ideal.
- **Small gardening tools** – a gardening fork, trowel and a watering can are useful.
- **Labels or lollysticks.**
- **Seed compost.** This can be bought from your local garden centre.

How to do it:
1 Spoon the compost into your pots.
2 Sprinkle the seeds into the pots, planting different herbs in different containers. Use plenty of seeds, as some may not grow. Lightly cover the newly planted seeds with compost. Label each pot with the herb's name or write it on a clean lolly stick and push it into the compost. Place the pots on to the tray.
3 Herbs need lots of sunlight to grow. Place your tray of pots on a sunny windowsill or other light place. As your plants grow, you can turn them around now and again so they get the light they need on all sides.
4 Water the seeds well straight away. From now on you will need to water them about once a week. Check the compost now and again to see if it is still moist, but do not put too much water in.
5 Wait. Water. And watch for the tiny green stalks pushing through the soil. This usually takes around 6–8 weeks. You can also fertilize your plants using an organic herb fertilizer.
6 When the herbs are grown, you can pinch off the leaves with your fingers and sprinkle them on to salads, or use them in recipes. The more you pinch off, the fuller and bushier your plants will grow. You can also move your herb plants to an outside spot if you wish.

Using your herbs

It's fun to smell and taste the different herbs. Which is your favourite?

Basil is great sprinkled on salads, on top of pizzas or made into pesto sauce for pasta.

Chives can be snipped off with scissors and scattered on top of potato salad.

Thyme sprigs are tasty additions to meat such as lamb or chicken and are good in stuffing.

Pizza paradise

Once you're a dab hand with herbs, why not try growing them by theme. How about a pizza garden? You'll need seeds for growing herbs that taste great scattered on pizza, e.g.

Basil
Thyme
Oregano
Rosemary
Parsley

Mint smells fantastic and can be used to make mint sauce – perfect with lamb.

Bunches of **lavender** smell lovely around the house and can be made into lavender bags to keep drawers smelling fresh.

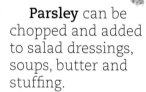

Parsley can be chopped and added to salad dressings, soups, butter and stuffing.

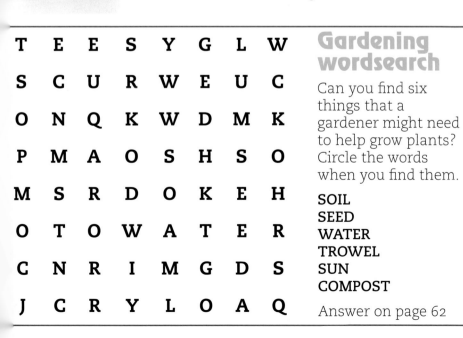

T	E	E	S	Y	G	L	W
S	C	U	R	W	E	U	C
O	N	Q	K	W	D	M	K
P	M	A	O	S	H	S	O
M	S	R	D	O	K	E	H
O	T	O	W	A	T	E	R
C	N	R	I	M	G	D	S
J	C	R	Y	L	O	A	Q

Gardening wordsearch

Can you find six things that a gardener might need to help grow plants? Circle the words when you find them.

SOIL
SEED
WATER
TROWEL
SUN
COMPOST

Answer on page 62

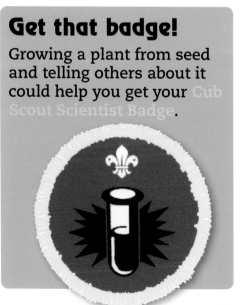

Get that badge!

Growing a plant from seed and telling others about it could help you get your Cub Scout Scientist Badge.

Things that fly

The Ancient Greeks told the story of Icarus, who flew using giant wings made of feathers and wax. But when he went too near the sun, the wax melted and Icarus plunged into the sea . . .

Throughout history, humans have tried to work out how to fly like a bird. Giant wings, flying machines, gliders – all kinds of ideas have been tried. Here are some of the successes:

- More than two thousand years ago the Chinese invented the kite – one of the first ever flying devices. The kites were made from bamboo and silk and were used in war to carry messages. Kite flying is still very popular in China.

- Leonardo da Vinci, the Italian inventor and artist, drew detailed sketches of a flying machine in 1483 (see below right). Though it was never actually built, it looked very much like a modern-day helicopter.

Humans have always looked to the skies and dreamed of flying.

- The Montgolfier brothers were the first humans to make a flight. They took off in their hot-air balloon in November 1783 and flew above Paris for 25 minutes. They caused a sensation!

- From 1799, a man called George Cayley designed many different gliders. He even built the first glider that could carry a human. But he realized that an engine would be needed to keep any kind of flying machine in the air for a long time.

- In 1903 Orville Wright flew the first powered plane, the Wright Flyer, in North Carolina, USA. That first flight lasted just twelve seconds, but during the following years, flying 'took off' in a big way. Many aeroplanes and engines were designed to transport people and cargo. Flying was here to stay!

Did you know?

In 2009, a Japanese man called Takuo Toda made a paper plane that stayed airborne for 27.9 seconds!

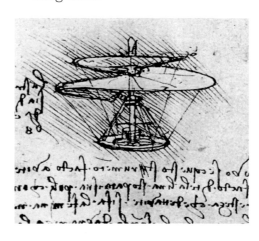

Get that badge!

Knowing about particular planes and telling your Pack about them can help you get a **Cub Scout Air Activities Activity Badge**. Making and flying paper planes will also help you.

Make a paper plane

This classic paper plane has been made and 'flown' by hundreds of children over the years. It's easy to make, so give it a try. All you need is an A4 piece of paper.

1 Fold your sheet of paper in half and open it out again.

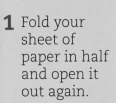

2 Fold the two top corners in to the centre fold and crease into triangles.

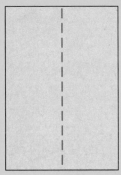

3 Fold the two outside corners in to the centre again.

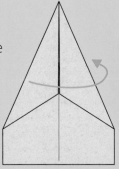

4 Turn the plane over.

5 Fold the right side over to the left.

6 Fold the wings down on both sides.

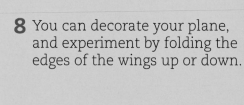

7 Now you have a paper plane! Hold it in the middle with the wings opened out – and throw!

8 You can decorate your plane, and experiment by folding the edges of the wings up or down.

Why don't you and your friends have a paper plane flying competition? Get everyone to make their own paper planes, then see how far they can fly. Write down the results!

Everest adventurers

Amazing Everest

- Everest is the world's highest and most famous mountain. It stands 8,850m (29,035ft) above sea level.
- It is part of a mountain range called the Himalayas, which are in Nepal, Asia.
- The very first ascent of Everest was made on 29 May 1953 by Sir Edmund Hillary and Tenzing Norgay.
- Thousands of people have climbed it since – but more than 200 deaths have been recorded.
- Mount Everest is a record-breaking mountain – and here are some record-breaking adventurers who have taken on the challenge.

Crevasse crisis!

In 1998, at the age of 23, our very own Chief Scout, Bear Grylls, became the youngest British climber to conquer Everest. He nearly didn't survive the expedition. As Bear was coming down the ice cracked open beneath him and he fell, knocking his head and becoming unconscious. When Bear came round he realized he was dangling from the end of his climbing rope – in a huge crevasse (a deep crack). Luckily, his teammate (and the rope!) saved his life.

Bear's British record was broken in 2011 by a young climber who made it to the peak of Everest just three days before his 17th birthday. George

Bear Grylls

Atkinson spent six weeks climbing Everest with a team. He not only broke the British record but gained another – the trip made him the youngest climber in the world to conquer

Climbing Everest is one of the biggest challenges an adventurer can face.

George Atkinson

the famous 'Seven Summits' – the tallest mountain peaks of each of the seven continents. One of those peaks is stunning Mount Kilimanjaro, in Africa, which George climbed at the age of 11.

World record – at 13!

Incredibly, in 2010, a young man from the USA, Jordan Romero, achieved his ambition of climbing Everest – at the age of 13! He now officially holds the record as the youngest person in the world to climb Everest.

Jordan was already a very experienced climber, having climbed six of the Seven Summits. He made the Everest expedition with his father, Paul, a mountaineer, his stepmother and three Sherpa guides. (Sherpas are people who come from the Himalayas.)

When he got to the top, Jordan rang his mum to tell her that he was literally 'on top of the world'!

53

Brave Bonita

Bonita Norris became the youngest British woman to conquer Everest, at the age of 22. It took her two years of tough fitness training and climbing to prepare for the mighty climb.

As with so many Everest climbs, there were a few problems along the way. On the descent Bonita slipped and badly injured her neck and shoulder. Luckily, she was rescued by a team of Sherpas who managed to help her back to safety.

What's next for Bonita? She plans to travel to both the North and the South Poles!

Things you should know about an Everest expedition

Climbing Everest is a risky business. Anyone making the attempt must be very fit and an experienced climber. He/she needs to be pretty brave too – and have a head for heights!

Possible dangers:

- The further you climb upwards, the less **oxygen** there is in the air. This can cause altitude sickness – making you feel very sick and unable to breathe or do anything properly. Climbers need to get used to the thin air and so it can take many weeks to complete an Everest expedition. Most climbers need to take bottles of oxygen with them to help them breathe.
- It is incredibly **cold** – temperatures can drop to minus 40 degrees. Climbers can lose limbs to frostbite and it is possible to die of the cold.
- Deadly **avalanches** sometimes occur. These are huge masses of snow and ice that suddenly tumble down a mountain, covering everything in their path.
- Vicious **snow storms** and ferocious **winds** can come out of nowhere, leaving climbers lost and freezing.
- One of the most dangerous stages of climbing Everest is the crossing of the Khumbu Icefall. This is a huge **glacier** in the lower parts of the mountain. It is full of deep crevasses that can only be crossed using a wobbly ladder. Huge pieces of ice – some as big as a house – can suddenly break off and fall because the glacier is constantly moving. It is a nerve-racking experience.

But, whatever the risk and danger, there are always more climbers who want to take on the challenge of the biggest mountain in the world!

What is a volcano? A mountain with hiccups!

Mountain Maze

Can you climb up to the peak of the mountain? Which way will you go? Watch out for dead ends!

BIG CLIMB brain teasers

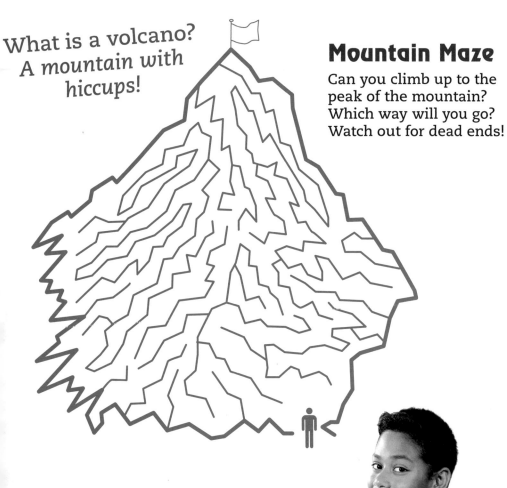

Why are mountain climbers so curious? They always want to take a peak!

Climber's Crossword

Complete the grid and you will find another word in the vertical box. It is something that climbers will see a lot of when they are on Everest!

1 On a long climb, you won't sleep in a bed but in a _____ ____ .

2 You will have to pitch one of these every night for your camp.

3 All climbers should tie this on to themselves in case they fall.

4 A strong one of these and you might get blown over!

What's in the rucksack?

Cross out any letters that you can see twice. Unscramble the letters that are left to find an important thing in this climber's rucksack.

— — —

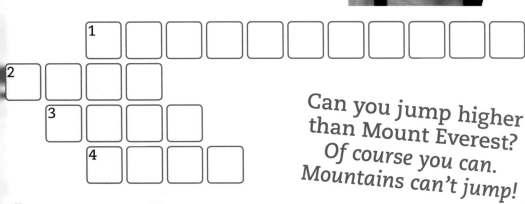

Can you jump higher than Mount Everest? Of course you can. Mountains can't jump!

All answers on page 62

Before Mount Everest was discovered, what was the highest mountain in the world?
Mount Everest – it was still the highest mountain even when it hadn't been discovered!

Fabulous

E very year Fundays are held at Gilwell Park near London, especially for Beaver and Cub Scouts. And every year thousands of girls and boys come along and have the time of their lives! With lots of activities to do, from robot wars to rafting, zip wiring to zorbing, it's a great chance to try something new and really challenge yourself. Just like these energetic Beavers and Cubs . . .

www.fundays.org.uk

Fundays!

What makes a fun day out for you?

The big quiz

Have you enjoyed reading your Cubs Annual? Did you find out lots of interesting facts along the way? Try our brilliant Big Quiz to see how much you can remember. If you don't know the answer, you will be able to find it somewhere in the book. Or just have a guess!

1 Which tree does this leaf come from?

a Oak tree ☐

b Horse chestnut tree ☐

c Silver birch tree ☐

2 Which bird is sacred in Japan?

a Kingfisher ☐

b Robin ☐

c Crane ☐

3 If you were out hiking, what would you be doing?

a Walking ☐

b Swimming ☐

c Skateboarding ☐

4 Which is the highest mountain in the world?

a Kilimanjaro ☐

b Everest ☐

c Snowdon ☐

5 Which creature buries acorns in the ground for the winter?

a Fox ☐

b Badger ☐

c Squirrel ☐

6 Which brothers first flew in a hot air balloon in 1783?

a Wright ☐

b Chuckle ☐

c Montgolfier ☐

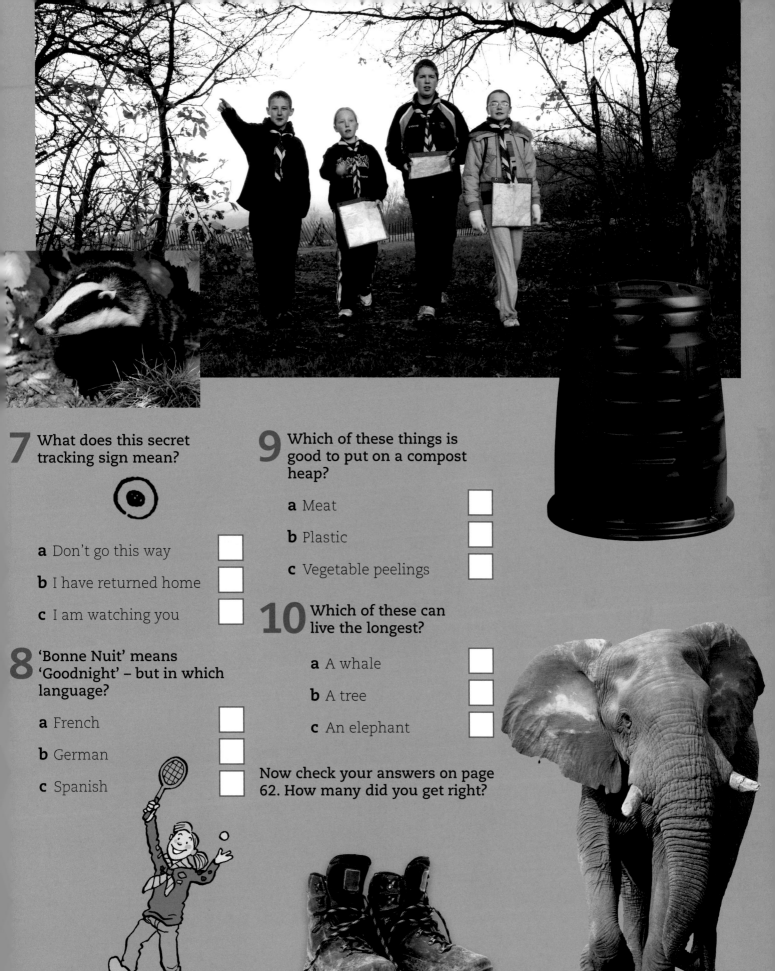

7 What does this secret tracking sign mean?

a Don't go this way ☐

b I have returned home ☐

c I am watching you ☐

8 'Bonne Nuit' means 'Goodnight' – but in which language?

a French ☐

b German ☐

c Spanish ☐

9 Which of these things is good to put on a compost heap?

a Meat ☐

b Plastic ☐

c Vegetable peelings ☐

10 Which of these can live the longest?

a A whale ☐

b A tree ☐

c An elephant ☐

Now check your answers on page 62. How many did you get right?

Win a BIG day out

It's competition time again and this year we are offering another brilliant prize for you and your Cub Scout Pack.

By answering a simple question you could win an amazing day out for 30 young people plus ten leaders to a Merlin attraction of your choice. Thanks to the generous folk at Merlin Groups, we have a mind-boggling choice of places you could visit if you are our lucky winner:

- The Alton Towers Resort
- LEGOLAND® Windsor
- Chessington World of Adventures Resort
- Madame Tussauds London and Blackpool
- The EDF Energy London Eye
- SEA LIFE centres & sanctuaries
- The London, Blackpool, York & Edinburgh Dungeon
- LEGOLAND® Discovery Centre Manchester
- The Blackpool Tower Attractions
- The Weymouth Tower
- Warwick Castle

All you need to do is answer this simple question:

How tall is Blackpool Tower?

As a tie breaker, please also tell us in 50 words or fewer **what you love most about being a Cub Scout**.

Please email your answer to **communications@scouts.org.uk** or put your answers on a postcard and send them to:

Cubs Annual 2013 Competition
**The Scout Association
Gilwell Park
Chingford
London
E4 7QW**

The closing date for entries is **31 March 2013**. Good luck!

Who won last year's competition?

Congratulations to Jacob, age 6, from 194th Kingswood Scout Group who won a fantastic trip to a Merlin theme park for him and his Colony. He correctly answered that LEGO means 'play well'.

'I love being a Beaver Scout,' said Jacob, 'because I can have lots of fun and get really messy without Mummy even knowing about it. I can go on sleepovers and stay up late and do lots of exciting things like going on torchlit walks and singing at campfires with lots of other Beavers, Cubs and Scouts.'

Information for leaders

Merlin Groups is part of The Merlin Entertainments Group offering group savings and benefits at 22 of the UK's Top Attractions.

Scouts can not only benefit from savings of over 50% off entry* and FREE leader and familiarization tickets but also the group has the opportunity to gain badges whilst visiting.

Let your group escape into a whole new adventure; we now offer camping experiences at the Alton Towers Resort, Chessington World of Adventures Resort and Warwick Castle.

To ensure your group finds out about all the latest news and offers sign up at **www.merlingroups.co.uk/win** and your group could win a FREE Group day out for up to 10 people to a Merlin Attraction of your choice!

Booking and advice

For further information and to book your day out please visit **www.merlingroups.com/scouts** or call 0871 222 6944.

LEGO, the LEGO logo and LEGOLAND are trademarks of the LEGO Group. © 2012 The LEGO Group.

Scouting – come and join the adventure!

Did you know that over 400,000 boys and girls across the UK enjoy the challenge and adventure of Scouting? Anyone aged 6–25 can join the Scouts and take part in exciting activities from abseiling to zorbing. Scouting is about fun, friendship and welcoming everyone, whatever their background, faith or culture. So if you're not involved already, why not come and join the adventure?

Brilliant Beavers

Beaver Scouts are boys and girls aged between 6 and 8. They meet up regularly and do lots of different things, such as playing games, learning about the outdoors and earning brilliant badges. Beaver Scouts wear a uniform and make a special

Promise when they join. If you're interested in becoming a Beaver Scout, find out where your local Colony meets and ask if you can go along one evening. You can find out how to become a member from the group leaders.

Cracking Cubs

Beavers go on to become Cub Scouts, who are aged 8–10½. You can join Cub Scouts in the three months leading up to your eighth birthday. At Cubs you can look forward to doing all the things that you did as a Beaver but with even more camps, interesting visits and outdoor fun. And badges, of course!

Once you have reached your tenth birthday, you might be thinking about moving from Cub Scouts into the third stage of the

great Scouting family – the Scouts themselves!

Super Scouts

At Scouts, you will still meet up, play games and make the same greetings and Scout sign. But, as you are now older and part of a Scout Troop, you can take part in even more grown-up and exciting activities such as Patrol projects, pioneering and longer camping expeditions. There is almost no limit to the fascinating and fun things you can do when you're a Scout!

For more information about Scouting and all the different badges and awards that young people can gain, go to www.scouts.org.uk

MY BADGES

SECRET ISLAND ADVENTURE

Download My Badges – The Scout Association's official badge app – and the game The Scouts: Secret Island Adventure available now from the App Store and as an Android app on Google Play.

Answers

Page 6: 1) oak 2) horse chestnut 3) beech 4) silver birch 5) sycamore 6) willow.

Page 8: Leaf Quiz. From top, clockwise: oak, willow, beech, horse chestnut, sycamore, silver birch.

Page 24: 1) 3G swing 2) trampolining 3) camping 4) rollerblading 5) orienteering 6) high ropes 7) rowing

Page 36: 1) skateboarding 2) ice skating 3) climbing wall 4) geocaching 5) mountain biking 6) skiing 7) hiking

Page 39: message reads 'Cubs are great!'

Page 40: message reads 'What's your name?'

Page 42 – Part 1: 1) three 2) yes 3) eating 4) two 5) red

Part 2: *Bonne nuit* = goodnight, *Danke* = thank you, *Perdon* = excuse me, *Fantastico* = great.

Part 4:

Part 5: *a bug* = a secret listening device, *shadowing* = secretly following someone, *safehouse* = a place where a spy can hide out, *a cover* = a false name.

Page 49: see right.

```
T E E S Y G L W
S C U R W E U C
O N Q K W D M K
P M A O S H S O
M S R D O K E H
O T O W A T E R
C N R I M G D S
J C R Y L O A Q
```

Page 55: Mountain Maze: see right. **What's in the rucksack?** MAP. **Climber's Crossword** 1) sleeping bag, 2) tent, 3) rope, 4) wind. The hidden word is SNOW.

Page 58: 1) a 2) c 3) a 4) b 5) c 6) c 7) b 8) a 9) c 10) b

Picture Credits

All photos © The Scout Association unless otherwise noted. Almostunschoolers.blogspot.com: page 16 middle right. Stuart Cox: pages 7, 18, 19, 32, 34–5, 46–7 and 48. Luca Galuzzi: page 52 main. Greg Goebel: page 50 middle. Marie in NC/Picasa: page 22. Bonita Norris: pages 54 top and 58 middle. Shutterstock.com: pages 5, 6, 8, 13, 16 top, middle left & bottom left, 17 top, 24 top, 25 middle left & bottom right, 26 bottom, 27, 30 left & middle, 31 top right, 36 top left & middle left, 37 middle left, 40 bottom left, 44, 45, 46 bottom left, 47 bottom left & middle, 48 bottom right, 49, 50 left & bottom, 51 bottom, 54 bottom, 55 bottom, 59 top left, bottom middle & right. SWNS.com: 53 left. Wikimedia Commons: page 50 top.

Grateful thanks are due to the following people: the Strauss family and www.myzerowaste.com page 17; Harvey Ward and the Broomwood Beaver Colony, Battersea page 20; Marie Gaffney, Ewan and friends from the 11th Fife/1st Burntisland Cub Pack page 20; Kim Thomas and the children of Saxon Hill School, Staffordshire page 21; Trish Parker and the 1st Wivenhoe Beaver Scout Colony page 21; Liz Pocknell and Eugene of the 1st Horsell Adventurers Beaver Colony, Woking District page 21.

All illustrations: David Parkins.

What was the best thing you did this year?

Draw yourself doing your favourite activity!

....

....

....

....

....

....

What badges did you earn?

....

....

....

What are you looking forward to next year?

....

....

....

....